The
CONT.
GARDENING

Everything You Need to Know to Start Growing Flowers, Herbs, and Vegetables in Small Places

By CHARLES LAINE

Copyright 2024 By CHARLES LAINE. All rights reserved.

No part of this publication may be reproduced, distributed, or transmitted in any form or by any means, including photocopying, recording, or other electronic or mechanical methods, without the prior written permission of the publisher, except in the case of brief quotations embodied in critical reviews and certain other noncommercial uses permitted by copyright law.

Contents

Introduction 4
Chapter 1: What is a Container Gardening 5
Chapter 2: The Basic Steps For Container Gardening 8
    Choosing the Right Containers 12
    Selecting Suitable Plants 16
    Tools And Equipment 20
Chapter 3: Container Maintenance 24
Chapter 4: Seasonal Container Gardening 26
    Winter season 27
    Summer Season 32
    Spring Season 39
    Autumn Season 44
Chapter 5: Container Gardening for Small Spaces: 49
Chapter 6: Creative Container Gardening Ideas: 60
Chapter 7: Common Container Gardening Issues 72
    Overwatering 72
    Underwatering 75
    Poor drainage 77
    Soil compaction 80
    Nutrient deficiency 82
    Root-Bound Plants 85
    Diseases 88
Conclusion 91

Introduction

Container gardening has emerged as a delightful and practical solution for individuals seeking to cultivate greenery and beauty in spaces of all shapes and sizes. Whether you reside in a bustling city apartment, a suburban home with limited outdoor space, or a sprawling countryside estate, container gardening offers a gateway to the natural world right at your fingertips. This gardening method transcends traditional boundaries, allowing enthusiasts to transform balconies, patios, rooftops, and indoor environments into vibrant havens teeming with life.

The allure of container gardening lies in its versatility, accessibility, and endless creative possibilities. With a simple container as your canvas and a selection of plants as your palette, you can craft personalized landscapes that reflect your tastes, preferences, and lifestyle. The options are virtually limitless, from aromatic herbs and bountiful vegetables to colorful flowers and ornamental shrubs.

This guide will explore the fundamentals of container gardening, from selecting the right containers and soil to choosing suitable plants, watering techniques, and maintenance tips. Whether you're a seasoned gardener looking to expand your horizons or a novice eager to embark on your green-thumb journey, this introduction to container gardening will equip you with the knowledge and inspiration to cultivate thriving and beautiful gardens in any space, big or small. So, roll up your sleeves, grab your trowel, and dive into the wonderful world of container gardening!

Chapter 1: What is a Container Gardening

Container gardening is growing plants in containers rather than directly in the ground. It's a flexible and versatile way to garden, suitable for spaces of all sizes, from large gardens to small balconies or even indoor environments. In container gardening, plants are grown in pots, planters, boxes, baskets, or any other container that can hold soil and have drainage holes.

Advantages

Space Efficiency: Container gardening allows people with limited space, such as apartment dwellers or those with small yards, to enjoy gardening. Containers can be placed on balconies, patios, rooftops, or indoors, making them accessible to urban and suburban gardeners.

Portability: Containers can be moved around easily, allowing gardeners to rearrange their space, follow the sun, or protect plants from harsh weather conditions. This flexibility is particularly useful for seasonal or tender plants indoors during the colder months.

Control Over Soil Quality: Container gardeners have full control over the soil composition, which can be tailored to suit the specific needs of different plants. This is especially advantageous for gardeners with poor soil quality in their outdoor space.

Pest and Weed Control: Container gardening can help reduce the risk of pests and weeds compared to traditional garden beds. Containers elevate plants above ground level, making them less accessible to pests, and can prevent weed seeds from infiltrating the soil.

Accessibility: Container gardening is accessible to people of all ages and physical abilities since it doesn't require bending or kneeling. Raised containers or elevated planters can bring plants to a more comfortable height for gardening.

Versatility and Creativity: With container gardening, the possibilities are endless. Gardeners can mix and match plants of different sizes, colors, and textures to create visually stunning displays. They can also experiment with unconventional containers, such as repurposed items or vertical gardens, to add interest to their space.

Common container plants include herbs, vegetables, flowers, shrubs, and small trees. Container gardens can thrive and provide a beautiful and productive oasis in any environment with proper care and attention to watering, fertilizing, and maintenance.

Chapter 2: The Basic Steps For Container Gardening

Container gardening offers endless possibilities for creativity, exploration, and enjoyment, allowing you to experience the rewards of gardening regardless of your available space or resources.

1. **Choosing the Right Containers:** Choose the right size, shape, and material for your plants and growing conditions. Consider factors such as drainage, insulation, and aesthetics when selecting containers for your garden. Ensure your containers have drainage holes at the bottom to prevent waterlogging and root rot.

2. **Choose the Right Potting Mix:** Select a high-quality potting mix for container gardening. Avoid using garden soil, which may contain pests, diseases, or weed seeds. Potting mixes are lightweight, well-draining, and nutrient-rich, providing an ideal growing environment for container plants.

3. **Plan Your Garden Layout:** Plan your garden layout before planting and decide which plants you want to grow in each container. Consider factors such as sunlight, water, and space requirements when selecting plants for your container garden. Arrange taller plants towards the center or back of the container, with trailing or cascading plants towards the edges.

4. **Prepare Containers for Planting:** Clean and disinfect your containers to remove any dirt, debris, or pathogens. Add a layer of drainage material, such as gravel or rocks, to the bottom of your containers to improve drainage. Fill containers with potting mix, leaving enough space at the top for planting.

5. **Plant Your Garden:** Once your containers are prepared, it's time to plant your garden. Gently remove plants from their nursery pots and place them in the containers, ensuring that the top of the root ball is level with the surface of the potting mix. Backfill around the roots with additional potting mix, firming gently to secure the plants in place.

6. **Water Thoroughly:** After planting, water your containers thoroughly to settle the potting mix around the roots and hydrate the plants. Water until excess moisture drains from the bottom of the container, ensuring that the potting mix is evenly moist throughout. Monitor soil moisture levels regularly and water as needed to keep the potting mix consistently moist but not waterlogged.

7. **Provide Adequate Sunlight:** Place your containers in a location that receives the appropriate amount of sunlight for your plants. To thrive, most vegetables, herbs, and flowering plants require at least 6-8 hours of direct sunlight daily. If you have limited sunlight, consider growing shade-tolerant plants or using artificial grow lights to supplement natural sunlight.

8. **Fertilize Regularly:** Container plants rely on you for their nutrients, so it's essential to fertilize them regularly throughout the growing season. Choose a balanced,

water-soluble fertilizer and follow the manufacturer's instructions for application. Fertilize plants every 2-4 weeks to ensure they have access to the essential nutrients they need for healthy growth.

9. **Monitor and Maintain:** Keep an eye on your container garden and monitor plants for signs of pests, diseases, or nutrient deficiencies. Prune away dead or diseased foliage, and promptly address pest infestations with organic or chemical treatments as needed. Regular maintenance, including watering, fertilizing, and pruning, will help keep your container garden healthy and thriving.

10. **Harvest and Enjoy:** As your container garden grows and matures, you'll be rewarded with a bountiful harvest of fresh herbs, vegetables, or flowers. Harvest crops when they are ripe and enjoy the fruits of your labor in delicious meals, beautiful bouquets, or simply by admiring the beauty of your garden oasis.

Choosing the Right Containers

Regarding container gardening, the variety of containers available is vast, offering gardeners numerous options to suit their preferences, space constraints, and aesthetic tastes. From traditional terracotta pots to modern hanging baskets, the choice of container can significantly impact the health and success of your plants.

Terracotta Pots

Terracotta pots are classic and timeless, made from porous clay that allows air and moisture to pass through. They provide excellent plant drainage but may dry out quickly, requiring more frequent watering. Terracotta pots come in various shapes and sizes, from small herb pots to large planters, and are suitable for indoor and outdoor use.

Plastic Pots

Plastic pots are lightweight, durable, and affordable, making them a popular choice for container gardening. They come in various colors, sizes, and styles, offering versatility and flexibility for gardeners. Plastic pots retain moisture well and are less prone to cracking or breaking than terracotta pots. They are ideal for both indoor and outdoor gardening.

Wooden Crates and Boxes

Wooden crates and boxes add rustic charm to container gardens and are perfect for growing vegetables, herbs, and flowers. They can be made from various types of wood, including cedar, pine, and redwood, and are available in different sizes and designs. Wooden containers provide good drainage and insulation for plants but may deteriorate over time if not properly treated or sealed.

Metal Containers

Metal containers, such as galvanized steel tubs, aluminum troughs, or wrought iron planters, add a modern and industrial aesthetic to container gardens. They are durable, weather-resistant, and come in various shapes and sizes. Metal containers may retain heat, so they are best suited for plants that can tolerate warmer temperatures.

Ceramic and Porcelain Pots

Ceramic and porcelain pots are elegant and stylish, often featuring intricate designs, patterns, and glazes. They are heavier than plastic or terracotta pots but provide excellent plant insulation. Ceramic and porcelain pots come in various sizes and colors, making them suitable for indoor and outdoor use.

Hanging Baskets

Hanging baskets are suspended from hooks or brackets and are perfect for adding vertical interest to gardens, patios, or balconies. They are typically made from plastic, wire, or woven fibers and come in various sizes and styles. Hanging baskets are ideal for trailing plants, such as ivy, ferns, or petunias, and require regular watering to prevent drying out.

Vertical Planters

Vertical planters are designed to maximize space by growing plants vertically rather than horizontally. They come in various configurations, including wall-mounted planters, tiered plant stands, and vertical gardening systems. Vertical planters are perfect for small spaces, such as balconies or patios, and can be used to create living walls or green screens.

Repurposed Containers

Gardeners can get creative with container gardening by repurposing everyday items such as buckets, barrels, tires, or old furniture. The possibilities are endless as long as the container has adequate drainage and is non-toxic to plants. Repurposed containers add character and personality to container gardens and are a sustainable and eco-friendly option for gardening.

When selecting containers for gardening, it's essential to consider factors such as drainage, insulation, durability, and aesthetics. Whether you prefer the traditional charm of terracotta pots or the modern elegance of ceramic planters, choosing the right container will help ensure the health and success of your container garden.

Selecting Suitable Plants

Choosing the right plants for container gardening is essential for creating a thriving and visually appealing garden. Unlike those grown in the ground, container plants have unique space, water, sunlight, and nutrient requirements. By selecting plants that are well-suited to container growing conditions, you can ensure the health and success of your garden. Some plants, like tomatoes and peppers, require full sun, while others, like ferns and certain herbs, thrive in partial shade.

Consider Sunlight Requirements

Before selecting plants for your container garden, assess the sunlight your garden receives throughout the day. Some plants, such as tomatoes, peppers, and herbs like basil and rosemary, thrive in full sun and require at least 6-8 hours of direct sunlight daily. Others, like ferns, coleus, and certain types of begonias, prefer partial shade and can tolerate less sunlight.

Choose Appropriate Container Sizes

Different plants have varying root systems and space requirements, so it's essential to choose containers that are the right size for your plants. Larger containers provide more room for root growth and help prevent plants from becoming root-bound, while smaller containers may restrict growth and require more frequent watering. Consider the mature size of the plants you intend to grow and select containers that accommodate their needs.

Select Plants with Similar Watering Needs

When planning your container garden, choose plants with similar watering requirements to make maintenance easier. Some plants, such as succulents, cacti, and lavender, prefer dry conditions and require infrequent watering, while others, like impatiens, ferns, and caladiums, prefer consistently moist soil. Grouping plants with similar watering needs in the same containers can help ensure that all plants receive the appropriate amount of water.

Think About Temperature Tolerance

Consider your area's climate and temperature fluctuations when choosing plants for container gardening. Some plants, such as tropicals like hibiscus, bougainvillea, and palms, thrive in warm temperatures and may need to be brought indoors during the colder months. Others, like pansies, ornamental cabbage, and certain grasses, are more cold-hardy and can tolerate cooler temperatures.

Choose Plants with Long Bloom Periods

To maximize your container garden's visual impact, select plants with long bloom periods or continuous flowering throughout the growing season. This ensures your garden remains vibrant and colorful for as long as possible. Plants like petunias, geraniums, marigolds, and zinnias are known for their prolific and extended blooming periods, making them popular choices for container gardens.

Consider Growth Habit and Size

Pay attention to the growth habit and size of the plants you choose, as this will determine how they fill out and interact with the container. Tall, upright plants, such as ornamental grasses, cannas, and dracaenas, add height and drama to container gardens while trailing or cascading plants, like trailing petunias, ivy, and sweet potato vines, spill over the edges of containers and soften the overall appearance.

Account for Maintenance Requirements

Consider the maintenance requirements of the plants you choose, including pruning, deadheading, and fertilizing. Some plants, such as roses, fuchsias, and dahlias, benefit from regular deadheading to promote continuous flowering, while others, like succulents and drought-tolerant plants, require minimal maintenance once established. Choose plants that align with your gardening style and available time for maintenance tasks.

Experiment with Plant Combinations

Don't be afraid to get creative and experiment with different plant combinations to create visually stunning container gardens. Mix and match plants with contrasting colors, textures, and heights to add interest and diversity to your garden. Consider incorporating a focal point plant, such as a tall grass or ornamental tree, surrounded by complementary flowers, foliage plants, and trailing vines for a dynamic and eye-catching display.

You can choose plants well-suited to container gardening and create a beautiful and thriving garden that brings joy and beauty to your indoor or outdoor space. With careful planning and consideration, you can enjoy a bountiful harvest of vegetables, a colorful display of flowers, or a lush oasis of greenery in your container garden.

Tools And Equipment

Container gardening requires specific tools and equipment to ensure efficient planting, maintenance, and care of plants in containers.

Containers

Choose pots, planters, or containers of various sizes and materials (e.g., terracotta, plastic, ceramic) based on your plants' specific needs and preferences. Ensure that containers have drainage holes to prevent waterlogging.

Potting Mix

Use a high-quality potting mix specifically formulated for container gardening. Avoid using garden soil, which can be too heavy and may contain pests or diseases.

Hand Trowel

A hand trowel is essential for planting, transplanting, and potting plants in containers. Choose a sturdy, ergonomic trowel for comfortable use.

Hand Pruners

Hand pruners are useful for trimming, pruning, and deadheading plants in containers. Look for sharp bypass pruners that can cut through stems cleanly without crushing them.

Watering Can or Hose

Ensure proper watering of container plants with a watering can or hose equipped with a nozzle attachment for gentle watering. Water plants thoroughly, allowing excess water to drain away from the containers.

Moisture Meter

A moisture meter helps monitor container soil moisture levels, preventing overwatering or underwatering. Insert the probe into the soil to determine when watering is needed.

Gloves

Protect your hands from thorns, sharp edges, and soil with gardening gloves. Choose gloves made of durable, breathable materials for comfort and protection.

Pruning Shears

Pruning shears or scissors are handy for trimming and shaping plants, removing dead or damaged foliage, and maintaining plant health in containers.

Fertilizer

Choose a balanced, water-soluble fertilizer specifically formulated for container plants. Follow the manufacturer's instructions for application rates and frequency to ensure proper plant nutrition.

Mulch

Apply a layer of organic mulch, such as shredded bark, straw, or compost, to the soil surface of containers to help retain moisture, suppress weeds, and regulate soil temperature.

Supports

Support tall or vining plants in containers with stakes, trellises, or cages to prevent them from leaning or toppling over as they grow.

Drip Trays

Place drip trays or saucers under containers to catch excess water runoff and prevent water damage to surfaces. Empty drip trays regularly to avoid waterlogging.

Soil Scoop or Hand Rake

Use a soil scoop or hand rake to loosen and aerate the potting mix, remove debris, and level the soil surface in containers.

Labels

Label containers with plant names, varieties, and planting dates to keep track of your container garden and maintain organized records.

Wheelbarrow or Garden Cart

Transport heavy containers, soil, and equipment easily using a wheelbarrow or garden cart. Choose a sturdy, lightweight model with pneumatic tires for smooth maneuverability.

The right tools and equipment will make container gardening more enjoyable and successful. Invest in high-quality tools and maintain them properly to ensure they last for many gardening seasons.

Chapter 3: Container Maintenance

Container gardening maintenance is essential for keeping your potted plants healthy, vibrant, and flourishing throughout the growing season. This ongoing process involves a series of tasks aimed at providing optimal care and addressing the needs of your container garden.

Watering

Proper watering is essential for container plants since they can't access moisture from the ground like plants in the garden. Check the soil's moisture level regularly by sticking your finger into the soil; if it feels dry an inch below the surface, it's time to water. Be mindful not to overwater, as this can lead to root rot. Aim to water in the morning to prevent evaporation loss and minimize the risk of fungal diseases.

Fertilizing

Container plants rely on you for their nutrients since their roots are confined to a limited space. Regularly fertilize your plants throughout the growing season with a balanced, water-soluble fertilizer to ensure they can access the essential nutrients they need to thrive.

Maintenance

Keep an eye out for pests and diseases, as container plants can be more susceptible to these issues due to their confined environment. Prune away dead or diseased foliage, and promptly address pest infestations with organic or chemical treatments as needed.

Seasonal Care

Container gardening allows you to change your plantings with the seasons, offering endless opportunities for creativity and experimentation. In colder climates, you can overwinter certain plants indoors or swap them out for cold-tolerant varieties. Conversely, in warmer climates, you can enjoy year-round gardening with diverse plants suited to your climate.

Chapter 4: Seasonal Container Gardening

Seasonal container gardening is a dynamic and rewarding way to refresh and rejuvenate your outdoor spaces throughout the year. By changing out plants and containers to suit the seasons, you can create visually stunning displays that reflect the beauty of each season and bring new life to your garden, patio, or balcony.

Winter season

Ideas For Winter Container Gardening

1. Winter Edible Container Gardening

Materials needed:

- Large outdoor containers with drainage holes
- Cold-hardy vegetables such as kale, spinach, arugula, lettuce, and Swiss chard
- Cold-tolerant herbs such as parsley, cilantro, chives, and thyme
- Potting soil
- Watering can or spray bottle
- Fertilizer (optional)

Steps:

1. Choose large outdoor containers suitable for winter planting with drainage holes in the bottom to prevent waterlogging. Consider using containers made of durable materials such as fiberglass, resin, or concrete that can withstand cold temperatures and harsh weather conditions.
2. Fill each container with potting soil, leaving a small space at the top for planting.
3. Mix cold-hardy vegetables and herbs to create a diverse and nutritious salad garden. Arrange the plants in each container, ensuring they are positioned securely and have enough room to grow.

4. Plant the vegetables and herbs in the containers, following the spacing and planting depth recommendations for each plant variety. Create a balanced and visually appealing arrangement by varying the plants' heights, textures, and colors.
5. Water the plants thoroughly after planting, ensuring the soil is evenly moist and not soggy. Use a watering can or spray bottle to water the plants gently, avoiding excessive splashing or runoff.
6. Place the containers in a sunny or partially shaded location on your patio, porch, or balcony where they can receive adequate sunlight for healthy growth and development. If your outdoor space doesn't receive enough sunlight, consider supplementing with grow lights.
7. Water the plants regularly throughout the winter, checking the soil moisture levels weekly and watering as needed to keep the soil evenly moist. Protect the containers from freezing temperatures and frost by moving them to a sheltered location or covering them with frost blankets or row covers.
8. Fertilize the plants every few weeks with a balanced liquid fertilizer to promote healthy growth and abundant harvests. Follow the manufacturer's instructions for application, and avoid over-fertilizing, which can lead to nutrient imbalances.
9. Harvest vegetables and herbs as they mature, snipping off leaves or stems as needed for fresh salads and culinary use. Harvesting regularly encourages new growth and helps maintain the shape and health of the plants.

Tips For Winter Container Gardening

Container gardening in the winter season requires some special attention to ensure the success of your plants despite the cold temperatures.

- Choose Cold-Hardy Plants: Select plants that are well-suited to the winter season and can withstand cold temperatures. Look for cold-hardy vegetables like kale, Swiss chard, spinach, and carrots and winter-blooming flowers like pansies, violas, and ornamental kale. These plants tolerate frost and chilly weather, making them ideal for winter container gardening.

- Use Insulating Containers: Choose containers from insulating materials such as thick ceramic, fiberglass, or double-walled plastic to help protect plant roots from freezing temperatures. Avoid materials like terracotta or metal, which can conduct cold and damage plant roots.

- Provide Adequate Drainage: Ensure your containers have drainage holes at the bottom to prevent waterlogging and root rot. Elevate containers slightly off the ground using pot feet or bricks to allow excess water to drain freely. Avoid placing containers directly on surfaces that can retain moisture, such as concrete or stone.

- Protect from Freezing: During periods of extreme cold, move your containers to a sheltered location, such as a porch, patio, or garage, to protect them from freezing temperatures and harsh winds. Cover containers with frost blankets, burlap, or old blankets to provide additional insulation and protect plants from frost damage.

- Water Wisely: Monitor soil moisture levels regularly and water your containers as needed to keep the soil evenly moist. During the winter, plants may require less frequent watering due to reduced evaporation rates and slower growth. Water in the morning to allow excess moisture to evaporate before temperatures drop in the evening, reducing the risk of frost damage.

- Mulch the Soil Surface: Apply a layer of mulch, such as shredded leaves, straw, or pine needles, to the soil surface of your containers to help insulate the roots and conserve soil moisture. Mulch also helps prevent soil erosion and suppresses weed growth, keeping your container garden healthy and thriving throughout the winter season.

- Protect from Frost Heaving: In regions with freezing and thawing cycles, protect container plants by insulating the soil surface with mulch or wrapping containers with insulating materials. Frost heaving occurs when soil repeatedly freezes and thaws, causing containers to shift and potentially damage plant roots.

- Monitor for Pests and Diseases: Keep an eye out for pests and diseases that may affect your container plants during winter. Inspect plants regularly for signs of damage or infestation and take prompt action to address any issues. Prune away dead or diseased foliage to maintain plant health and vigor.

- Harvest Continuously: Continue harvesting winter vegetables and herbs as needed throughout the season to encourage new growth and ensure the health of your plants. Regular harvesting also prevents plants from becoming overcrowded and encourages air circulation, reducing the risk of pests and diseases.

- Rotate Containers: Rotate containers periodically to ensure that all sides of the plants receive adequate sunlight and airflow. This helps promote even growth and prevents plants from becoming leggy or unevenly shaped. Rotate containers every few weeks to ensure all plants receive equal exposure to sunlight and airflow.

Summer Season

Ideas For Summer Container Gardening

1. Succulent Container Gardening
Materials needed:

- Large outdoor container with drainage holes
- Assorted succulent plants such as echeverias, sedums, aeoniums, and agaves
- Cacti varieties such as barrel cacti, bunny ears cacti, or prickly pears
- Succulent potting mix or well-draining soil
- Decorative rocks or gravel
- Watering can or spray bottle (for initial watering)
- Optional: Slow-release fertilizer

Steps:

1. Choose a large outdoor container with plenty of drainage holes to prevent waterlogging. Select a container with enough space to accommodate multiple succulent and cacti varieties, allowing for growth and expansion over time.
2. Fill the container with succulent potting mix or well-draining soil, leaving a few inches of space at the top for planting and watering.
3. Arrange the assorted succulent plants and cacti in the container, considering their size, shape, and growth

habits. Create a visually appealing landscape by varying the plants' heights, textures, and colors.
4. Plant the succulents and cacti in the container, ensuring they are positioned securely and have enough room to grow. Add additional soil around the plants as needed to stabilize them.
5. Once the plants are in place, top-dress the container with decorative rocks or gravel to help retain moisture and prevent soil erosion. This also adds a finishing touch to your succulent landscape.
6. Water the succulents and cacti thoroughly after planting, allowing the water to soak into the soil and reach the roots. Use a watering can or spray bottle to water the plants gently, avoiding excessive splashing or runoff.
7. Place the container in a sunny location where the succulents and cacti can receive at least 6-8 hours of sunlight daily. Ensure the container has proper airflow to prevent moisture buildup and rot.
8. Water the succulents and cacti sparingly throughout the summer, allowing the soil to dry out between waterings. Succulents and cacti are drought-tolerant plants and prefer dry conditions, so be cautious not to overwater.
9. Optional: Apply a slow-release fertilizer to the container once or twice during summer to provide nutrients for healthy growth and vibrant colors. Follow the manufacturer's instructions for application.

2. Herb Container Gardening

Materials needed:

- Large outdoor containers with drainage holes
- Assorted herb plants or seeds (such as basil, parsley, cilantro, thyme, rosemary, and mint)
- Potting soil
- Watering can or spray bottle
- Fertilizer (optional)

Steps:

1. Choose large outdoor containers suitable for summer herb gardening with drainage holes in the bottom to prevent waterlogging. Consider using containers made of durable materials such as fiberglass, resin, or terra cotta.
2. Fill each container with potting soil, leaving a few inches of space at the top for planting and watering.
3. Select various herb plants or seeds you'd like to grow in your culinary herb garden. Consider choosing herbs that thrive in warm weather and are commonly used in cooking.
4. Plant the herb plants or sow the herb seeds in the containers, following the spacing and planting depth recommendations for each herb variety. Arrange the herbs according to your desired design and culinary preferences.
5. Water the herb plants thoroughly after planting, ensuring that the soil is evenly moist but not waterlogged. Use a watering can or spray bottle to water the plants gently, avoiding excessive splashing or runoff.

6. Place the containers in a sunny location on your patio, balcony, or deck where they can receive at least 6-8 hours of sunlight daily. Herbs typically prefer full sun, so choose a spot with plenty of direct sunlight during summer.
7. Water the herb plants regularly throughout the summer, checking the soil moisture levels weekly and watering as needed to keep the soil evenly moist. Herbs prefer consistently moist soil but can tolerate brief periods of dryness between waterings.
8. Optional: Apply a balanced liquid fertilizer to the containers every few weeks to promote healthy growth and abundant foliage. Follow the manufacturer's instructions for application, and avoid over-fertilizing, which can lead to nutrient imbalances.
9. Harvest herbs as they mature, snipping off leaves or stems as needed for fresh culinary use. Harvesting regularly encourages new growth and helps maintain the shape and health of the plants.

Tips For Summer Container Gardening

Container gardening in the summer presents challenges and considerations, particularly regarding heat and water management.

- Choose Heat-Tolerant Plants: Choose plants well-suited to hot and sunny conditions, such as succulents, drought-tolerant annuals like zinnias and portulaca, and heat-loving herbs like rosemary and lavender. These plants can better withstand the high temperatures and intense sunlight of summer.

- Use Large Containers: Opt for larger containers that provide more soil volume and better insulation for plant roots. Larger containers also hold moisture better than smaller ones, reducing watering frequency during hot summer days. Choose containers made from ceramic or thick plastic that provide insulation against heat.

- Ensure Adequate Drainage: Proper drainage is essential to prevent waterlogged soil, root rot, and other moisture-related issues. Ensure that your containers have drainage holes at the bottom, and use a well-draining potting mix to promote healthy root growth. Elevate containers on pot feet or bricks to improve drainage and airflow.

- Water Frequently: Water your container garden regularly, especially during hot and dry weather. Containers tend to dry out more quickly than garden beds, so check soil moisture levels daily and water as needed to keep the soil evenly moist. Water deeply until water drains from the bottom of the container, ensuring that plant roots receive an adequate water supply.

- Mulch the Soil Surface: Apply a layer of organic mulch, such as shredded bark or compost, to the soil surface of your containers to help conserve moisture, suppress weed growth, and regulate soil temperature. Mulch also helps prevent soil erosion and reduces evaporation, allowing you to water less frequently.

- Provide Shade: Shield your containers from the harsh midday sun by placing them in a location that receives morning or afternoon sun and partial shade during the hottest part of the day. Position containers under trees, awnings, and pergolas, or use shade cloth to protect from intense sunlight and heat.

- Fertilize Regularly: Feed your container plants a balanced, water-soluble fertilizer every 2-4 weeks during the growing season to provide essential nutrients for healthy growth and blooming. Follow the manufacturer's instructions for application, and avoid over-fertilizing, which can lead to nutrient imbalances and burn plant roots.

- Deadhead and Prune: Remove spent flowers and prune away dead or yellowing foliage regularly to encourage continuous blooming and maintain plant health. Deadheading redirects energy back into the plant and promotes new growth and flowering, keeping your container garden neat and vibrant throughout the summer.

- Monitor for Pests and Diseases: Look for common pests and diseases that can affect container plants during the summer months, such as aphids, spider mites, powdery mildew, and fungal infections. Inspect plants regularly for signs of damage or infestation and take prompt action to address any issues.

- Support for Tall Plants: Stake or support tall or sprawling plants to prevent them from toppling over or becoming damaged by wind or heavy rain. Use bamboo stakes, trellises, or tomato cages to support plants like tomatoes, peppers, and flowering vines, ensuring they remain upright and stable throughout summer.

Spring Season

Ideas For Spring Container Gardening

1. Colorful Spring Flower Garden
Materials needed:

- Large outdoor containers with drainage holes
- Assorted early-blooming annual flowers such as pansies, violas, primroses, and snapdragons
- Early-blooming perennial flowers such as tulips, daffodils, hyacinths, and crocuses
- Potting soil
- Watering can or spray bottle
- Fertilizer (optional)

Steps:

1. Choose large outdoor containers suitable for spring flower gardening with drainage holes in the bottom to prevent waterlogging. Consider using containers made of durable materials such as fiberglass, resin, or terra cotta.
2. Fill each container with potting soil, leaving a few inches of space at the top for planting and watering.
3. Select a mix of early-blooming annual and perennial flowers that will thrive in the cool temperatures of spring. Choose colors, shapes, and sizes to create a vibrant, eye-catching display.
4. Plant the annual and perennial flowers in the containers, following the spacing and planting depth

recommendations for each plant variety. Arrange the flowers according to your desired design and color scheme, ensuring they are positioned securely and have enough room to grow.
5. Water the flower plants thoroughly after planting, ensuring the soil is evenly moist but not soggy. Use a watering can or spray bottle to water the plants gently, avoiding excessive splashing or runoff.
6. Place the containers in a sunny or partially shaded location on your patio, balcony, or deck where they can receive adequate sunlight for healthy growth and flowering. Ensure that the containers have proper airflow to prevent moisture buildup and rot.
7. Water the flower plants regularly throughout spring, checking the soil moisture levels weekly and watering as needed to keep the soil evenly moist. Protect the containers from frost and freezing temperatures by moving them to a sheltered location or covering them with frost blankets or row covers.
8. Optional: Apply a balanced liquid fertilizer to the containers every few weeks to promote healthy growth and abundant flowering. Follow the manufacturer's instructions for application, and avoid over-fertilizing, which can lead to nutrient imbalances.
9. Deadhead faded flowers regularly to encourage continuous blooming and maintain the overall appearance of the containers. Remove any dead or yellowing foliage to promote new growth and prevent disease.

Tips For Spring Container Gardening

Container gardening in the spring is exciting as plants awaken from dormancy and new growth emerges.

- Plan Your Garden: Plan your container garden layout and choose plants that thrive in the springtime climate. Consider sunlight exposure, water requirements, and mature plant size when selecting plants for your containers. Create a planting scheme incorporating a mix of spring-blooming flowers, foliage plants, and edible crops for a diverse and vibrant display.

- Choose Early-Blooming Plants: Select plants that bloom early in the spring to kick-start your container garden with color and fragrance. Look for spring-flowering bulbs such as tulips, daffodils, hyacinths, crocuses, and early-blooming perennials like primroses, pansies, and violas. These plants will give your containers an instant burst of color and beauty as the weather warms up.

- Prepare Containers: Clean and disinfect your containers from the previous growing season to remove debris, pests, or diseases. Check containers for drainage holes and ensure they are in good condition for planting. Fill containers with fresh potting mix, adding organic matter or slow-release fertilizer to provide nutrients for growing plants.

- Plant Cool-Season Vegetables: Take advantage of the cooler temperatures of early spring to grow cool-season vegetables and herbs in your containers. Plant crops like lettuce, spinach, kale, radishes, peas, and herbs such as parsley, cilantro, and chives. These plants will thrive in the milder weather and provide fresh harvests for your kitchen table.

- Protect from Late Frosts: Keep an eye on the weather forecast and be prepared to protect your container garden from late frosts and cold snaps. Cover containers with frost blankets, row covers, or plastic sheeting to provide insulation and protect tender plants from frost damage. If frost is imminent, move containers to a sheltered location, such as a porch or patio.

- Water Regularly: As temperatures rise and plants grow actively, water your container garden regularly to moisten the soil. Check soil moisture levels daily and water as needed, especially during dry spells or windy weather. Water early in the day to minimize evaporation and ensure plants can access moisture when needed.

- Fertilize as Needed: Feed your container plants a balanced, water-soluble fertilizer to provide essential nutrients for healthy growth and blooming. Follow the manufacturer's instructions for application and adjust fertilization rates based on plant needs and container size. Avoid over-fertilizing, which can lead to nutrient imbalances and burn plant roots.

- Monitor for Pests and Diseases: Keep an eye out for common pests and diseases that can affect container plants in the spring, such as aphids, slugs, snails, and fungal infections. Inspect plants regularly for signs of damage or infestation and take prompt action to address any issues. Remove affected leaves or treat plants with organic or chemical controls as needed.

- Deadhead and Prune: Remove spent flowers and prune back leggy growth regularly to encourage new growth and prolong the blooming period of your spring-flowering plants. Deadheading redirects energy back into the plant and promotes continued blooming, keeping your container garden neat and tidy throughout spring.

Autumn Season

Ideas For Autumn Container Gardening

1. Harvest-Themed Container Garden

Materials needed:

- Large outdoor containers with drainage holes
- Seasonal plants such as ornamental kale, chrysanthemums, pansies, and ornamental grasses
- Autumn foliage, such as colorful leaves, branches, and berries
- Decorative accents such as pumpkins, gourds, cornstalks, and scarecrows
- Potting soil
- Watering can or spray bottle
- Fertilizer (optional)

Steps:

1. Choose large outdoor containers suitable for autumn gardening with drainage holes in the bottom to prevent waterlogging. Consider using containers made of durable materials such as fiberglass, resin, or terra cotta.
2. Fill each container with potting soil, leaving a few inches of space at the top for planting and watering.
3. Select a mix of seasonal plants, foliage, and decorative accents that will evoke the colors and textures of autumn. Choose plants with foliage that turn shades of red, orange, yellow, and burgundy, and incorporate decorative

elements such as pumpkins, gourds, and cornstalks for added visual interest.
4. Plant the seasonal plants and foliage in the containers, arranging them according to your desired design and color scheme. Ensure that the plants are positioned securely and have enough room to grow.
5. Add decorative accents like pumpkins, gourds, and cornstalks to the containers to enhance the harvest-themed theme. Arrange the accents around the plants and foliage, creating a cohesive and visually appealing display.
6. Water the plants and foliage thoroughly after planting, ensuring the soil is evenly moist but not waterlogged. Use a watering can or spray bottle to water the plants gently, avoiding excessive splashing or runoff.
7. Place the containers in a sunny or partially shaded location on your patio, balcony, or deck where they can receive adequate sunlight for healthy growth and development. Ensure that the containers have proper airflow to prevent moisture buildup and rot.
8. Water the plants and foliage regularly throughout the autumn, checking the soil moisture levels weekly and watering as needed to keep the soil evenly moist. Protect the containers from frost and freezing temperatures by moving them to a sheltered location or covering them with frost blankets or row covers.
9. Optional: Apply a balanced liquid fertilizer to the containers every few weeks to promote healthy growth and vibrant foliage. Follow the manufacturer's instructions for application, and avoid over-fertilizing, which can lead to nutrient imbalances.

Tips For Autumn Container Gardening

Choose Fall-Blooming Plants: Select plants that thrive in cooler temperatures and offer vibrant fall colors or blooms. Consider incorporating fall-blooming annuals such as chrysanthemums, pansies, ornamental kale, asters, and perennials like sedum, ornamental grasses, and autumn crocus.

- Plant Cool-Season Vegetables: Take advantage of the cooler temperatures of autumn to grow cool-season vegetables and herbs in your containers. Plant crops like lettuce, spinach, kale, Swiss chard, arugula, radishes, carrots, and herbs such as parsley, cilantro, and chives. These plants will thrive in the milder weather and provide fresh harvests well into the fall.

- Transition Summer Plants: As summer annuals fade, replace them with fall-blooming or cool-season plants to refresh your container garden for autumn. Remove spent flowers and trim back leggy growth to encourage new growth and prolong the blooming period of your summer plants.

- Add Seasonal Accents: Incorporate seasonal accents such as pumpkins, gourds, ornamental corn, and decorative grasses to add a festive touch to your container garden. Arrange these elements around your plants or use them as focal points to create eye-catching displays that celebrate the spirit of autumn.

- Consider Fall Color Schemes: Choose containers and plants with colors that complement the natural hues of autumn, such as warm shades of red, orange, yellow, and burgundy. Mix and match plants with different foliage textures and colors to create visual interest and depth in your container arrangements.

- Protect from Frost: Monitor weather forecasts and take steps to protect your container garden from early frosts and chilly nights. Move containers to a sheltered location, such as a porch or patio, or cover them with frost blankets or row covers to provide insulation and protect plants from frost damage.

- Mulch and Insulate: Apply a layer of mulch to the soil surface of your containers to help insulate plant roots and conserve moisture. Use organic mulches like shredded leaves, straw, or compost to regulate soil temperature and reduce moisture loss through evaporation. Mulching also helps suppress weed growth and improve soil structure.

- Water Wisely: Adjust your watering schedule as temperatures cool and rainfall increases in autumn. Water plants as needed to keep the soil evenly moist, but be mindful of excess moisture and waterlogging, especially in containers with poor drainage. Monitor soil moisture levels regularly and water early in the day to allow excess moisture to evaporate before temperatures drop at night.

- Maintain and Prune: Maintain your container garden by deadheading spent flowers, removing yellowing foliage, and pruning back overgrown or leggy growth. Pruning encourages new growth and helps maintain the shape and health of your plants throughout the autumn season.

- Harvest Edibles: Harvest ripe fruits, vegetables, and herbs from your container garden as they mature, enjoying the bounty of the autumn harvest. Harvesting regularly encourages continued production and ensures your plants remain healthy and productive throughout the season.

Chapter 5: Container Gardening for Small Spaces:

1. Herb Garden Using A Hanging Shoe Organizer

This vertical herb garden is an excellent solution for small spaces such as apartments, condos, or urban balconies, where space constraints may limit traditional gardening. By utilizing vertical space and repurposing a hanging shoe organizer, you can create a compact and productive herb garden that provides fresh herbs for cooking while adding greenery and beauty to your living space.

Materials needed:

- Hanging shoe organizer with pockets
- Herb plants or seeds (such as basil, parsley, cilantro, thyme, or rosemary)
- Potting soil
- Watering can or spray bottle
- Sunlight or grow lights

Steps:

1. Hang the shoe organizer on a sturdy hook or rod in a sunny location, such as a balcony railing, patio fence, or kitchen wall.
2. Fill each shoe organizer pocket with potting soil, leaving a small space at the top for planting herbs.
3. Plant herb seeds or transplant herb seedlings into each pocket, following the spacing and planting depth recommendations for each herb variety.
4. Water the soil in each pocket thoroughly using a watering can or spray bottle, ensuring that the soil is evenly moist but not waterlogged.
5. Place the shoe organizer in a location where it receives at least 6-8 hours of sunlight per day, or supplement with grow lights if natural light is limited.
6. Monitor the soil's moisture levels regularly and water the herbs as needed to keep the soil evenly moist.
7. Harvest herbs as they mature, snipping off leaves or stems as needed for culinary use.

8. Rotate the shoe organizer periodically to ensure all herbs receive adequate sunlight and airflow.
9. Enjoy fresh herbs from your vertical herb garden, adding flavor and freshness to your meals while maximizing space in your small outdoor or indoor area.

2. Hanging Garden On A Balcony

Materials needed:

- Hanging baskets or planters
- Potting soil
- Assorted flowering plants or trailing vines
- Watering can or spray bottle
- Fertilizer (optional)
- Hooks or brackets for hanging

Steps:

1. Choose hanging baskets or planters for your balcony space and aesthetic preferences. Consider using baskets with built-in liners or pots with drainage holes to prevent waterlogging.
2. Fill each hanging basket or planter with potting soil, leaving a small space at the top for planting.
3. Select various flowering plants or trailing vines that will thrive in your balcony's sunlight conditions and climate. Consider using a mix of annuals and perennials for season-long color.
4. Plant the flowers or vines in the hanging baskets or planters, arranging them according to your desired design and spacing. Ensure that the plants are positioned securely and have enough room to grow and trail over the edges of the containers.
5. Water the plants thoroughly after planting, ensuring the soil is evenly moist and not soggy. Use a watering can or spray bottle to water the plants gently, avoiding excessive splashing or runoff.
6. Hang the filled baskets or planters from hooks or brackets attached to the balcony railing, wall, or ceiling. Ensure that the hooks or brackets are securely anchored and can support the weight of the containers and plants.
7. Place the hanging baskets or planters in a sunny or partially shaded location on your balcony, where they can receive adequate sunlight for healthy growth and flowering.
8. Water the plants regularly, checking the soil moisture levels daily and watering as needed to keep the soil evenly moist. Use a balanced liquid fertilizer every few

weeks to promote healthy growth and abundant flowering.

9. Monitor the plants for signs of pests, diseases, or nutrient deficiencies, and take prompt action to address any issues. Remove faded flowers and dead foliage regularly to encourage continuous blooming and maintain the overall health of the plants.
10. Enjoy the beauty and fragrance of your hanging garden as it fills your balcony with color, texture, and life. Sit back, relax, and take pride in your container gardening efforts as you create a tranquil and inviting outdoor oasis on your balcony.

3. Colorful Window Box Garden

Materials needed:

- Window box planter with drainage holes
- Potting soil
- Assorted flowering plants or seeds
- Watering can or spray bottle
- Fertilizer (optional)
- Saucers or trays to catch excess water

Steps:

1. Choose a window box planter that fits the width and length of your windowsill and has drainage holes in the bottom to prevent waterlogging.
2. Fill the window box planter with potting soil, leaving a small space at the top for planting.
3. Select various flowering plants or seeds you'd like to grow in your window box garden. Consider using a mix of annuals and perennials for season-long color and interest.
4. Plant the flowering plants or sow the flowering seeds in the window box planter, following the spacing and planting depth recommendations for each plant variety. Arrange the plants according to your desired design and color scheme, ensuring they are positioned securely and have enough room to grow.
5. Water the plants thoroughly after planting, ensuring the soil is evenly moist and not soggy. Use a watering can or spray bottle to water the plants gently, avoiding excessive splashing or runoff.
6. Place the window box planter on your windowsill, positioning it in a sunny or partially shaded location where it can receive adequate sunlight for healthy growth and flowering. If your windowsill doesn't receive enough sunlight, consider choosing flowering plants that thrive in partial shade.
7. Water the plants regularly, checking the soil moisture levels daily and watering as needed to keep the soil evenly moist. Empty any excess water from the saucers or trays to prevent waterlogging.
8. Fertilize the flowering plants every few weeks with a balanced liquid fertilizer to promote healthy growth and

abundant blooming. Follow the manufacturer's instructions for application, and avoid over-fertilizing, which can lead to nutrient imbalances.
9. Deadhead faded flowers regularly to encourage continuous blooming and maintain the overall appearance of the window box garden. Remove any dead or yellowing foliage to promote new growth and prevent disease.
10. Enjoy the beauty and fragrance of your colorful window box garden as it fills your windowsill with vibrant blooms and adds charm and curb appeal to your home. Sit back, relax, and take pride in your flower container gardening efforts as you create a cheerful and welcoming outdoor oasis on your windowsill.

4. Vertical Salad Garden For Balcony

Materials needed:

- Hanging planters or vertical garden system
- Potting soil
- Assorted leafy greens such as lettuce, spinach, arugula, and kale
- Herbs such as basil, parsley, cilantro, and chives
- Watering can or drip irrigation system
- Fertilizer (optional)

Steps:

1. Choose hanging planters or a vertical garden system that is suitable for balcony gardening and can be securely attached to the balcony railing, wall, or ceiling. Consider using lightweight materials such as fabric or plastic for hanging planters or modular systems that can be easily assembled and customized.
2. Fill each planter or module with potting soil, ensuring enough space for planting and root growth. Use a high-quality potting mix that is well-draining and nutrient-rich to support healthy plant growth.
3. Select a variety of leafy greens and herbs that are well-suited to container gardening and thrive in the limited space of a balcony. Choose compact or dwarf varieties that don't require much space to grow and can tolerate the confined environment of a container.
4. Plant the leafy greens and herbs in the hanging planters or vertical garden system, following the spacing and planting depth recommendations for each plant variety.

Arrange the plants according to your desired design and culinary preferences, ensuring they are positioned securely and have enough room to grow.

5. Water the plants thoroughly after planting, ensuring the soil is evenly moist and not soggy. Use a watering can or drip irrigation system to water the plants gently, taking care not to overwater or saturate the soil.

6. Hang the planters or vertical garden system in a sunny location on your balcony where the leafy greens and herbs can receive at least 6-8 hours of sunlight daily. If your balcony doesn't receive enough sunlight, consider supplementing with grow lights or choosing plants that tolerate partial shade.

7. Water the plants regularly throughout the growing season, checking the soil moisture levels weekly and watering as needed to keep the soil evenly moist. Use a moisture meter or finger to gauge soil moisture and adjust watering accordingly.

8. Optional: Apply a balanced liquid fertilizer to the plants every few weeks to promote healthy growth and abundant foliage. Follow the manufacturer's instructions for application, and avoid over-fertilizing, which can lead to nutrient imbalances.

9. Harvest leafy greens and herbs as they mature, snipping off leaves or stems as needed for fresh salads, sandwiches, and culinary use. Harvesting regularly encourages new growth and helps maintain the shape and health of the plants.

Chapter 6: Creative Container Gardening Ideas:

1. Household items

The creative container gardening idea is repurposing household items as planters, giving your garden a unique and personalized touch.

Materials needed:

- Various household items for repurposing (e.g., old teapots, colanders, boots, tires, wooden crates, tin cans, watering cans, or even old furniture)
- Potting soil
- Assorted plants or seeds
- Drill (if necessary)
- Waterproof sealant (if necessary)
- Watering can or spray bottle
- Fertilizer (optional)

Steps:

1. Gather a selection of household items you'd like to repurpose as planters for your container garden. Get creative and think outside the box—almost anything can be turned into a planter with a little imagination!
2. Prepare the chosen items for planting. If necessary, drill drainage holes in the bottom of the containers to allow excess water to escape and prevent waterlogging. For non-porous items like teapots or watering cans, you may need to apply a waterproof sealant to prevent water damage.
3. Fill each repurposed container with potting soil, leaving a few inches of space at the top for planting and watering.
4. Select various plants or seeds suitable for container gardening and will thrive in the size and shape of your repurposed containers. Choose plants with similar light and water requirements to ensure they will grow well together.

5. Plant the selected plants or sow the seeds in the repurposed containers, following the spacing and planting depth recommendations for each plant variety. Arrange the plants creatively, considering the shape and size of the containers and their aesthetic appeal.
6. Water the plants thoroughly after planting, ensuring the soil is evenly moist and not soggy. Use a watering can or spray bottle to water the plants gently, avoiding excessive splashing or runoff.
7. Place the repurposed containers in a sunny or partially shaded location where the plants can receive adequate sunlight for healthy growth. Arrange the containers in groups or clusters to create visual interest and maximize space.
8. Water the plants regularly throughout the growing season, checking the soil moisture levels weekly and watering as needed to keep the soil evenly moist. Use a moisture meter or finger to gauge soil moisture and adjust watering accordingly.
9. Optional: Apply a balanced liquid fertilizer to the plants every few weeks to promote healthy growth and abundant flowering. Follow the manufacturer's instructions for application, and avoid over-fertilizing, which can lead to nutrient imbalances.

2. Old wooden pallets

The creative container gardening idea is to use old wooden pallets as vertical planters.

Materials needed:

- Wooden pallet
- Landscape fabric or plastic sheeting
- Potting soil
- Assorted plants or seeds
- Drill (optional)
- Screws or nails
- Hammer or screwdriver

- Watering can or spray bottle
- Fertilizer (optional)

Steps:

1. Find an old wooden pallet that is in good condition and free from chemical treatments or contaminants. Choose a pallet with slats wide enough to accommodate plants and soil.
2. Prepare the wooden pallet for planting by lining the back and sides with landscape fabric or plastic sheeting to hold the soil in place and prevent it from falling out.
3. Fill each pallet section with potting soil, pressing it down gently to ensure it is firmly packed and won't spill out. Leave a few inches of space at the top for planting and watering.
4. Select a variety of plants or seeds that are suitable for vertical gardening and will thrive in the conditions of your outdoor space. Consider using trailing plants like ivy or petunias for a cascading effect.
5. Plant the selected plants or sow the seeds in the pockets of soil within the pallet, spacing them evenly and arranging them creatively to maximize visual appeal.
6. Secure the plants by gently pressing the soil around the roots and patting it down to ensure they are stable and won't fall out.
7. Hang the pallet vertically on a sturdy wall or fence using screws or nails, ensuring it is securely attached and won't come loose. Alternatively, lean the pallet against a wall or fence for a more rustic look.
8. Water the plants thoroughly after planting, ensuring the soil is evenly moist and not soggy. Use a watering can or

spray bottle to water the plants gently, taking care not to overwater.
9. Place the pallet in a sunny or partially shaded location where the plants can receive adequate sunlight for healthy growth. Water the plants regularly throughout the growing season, checking the soil moisture levels weekly and watering as needed to keep the soil evenly moist.
10. Optional: Apply a balanced liquid fertilizer to the plants every few weeks to promote healthy growth and vibrant foliage. Follow the manufacturer's instructions for application, and avoid over-fertilizing, which can lead to nutrient imbalances.
11. Enjoy your vertical pallet planter's unique and space-saving beauty as it transforms an ordinary wall or fence into a lush green oasis. Sit back, relax, and take pride in your gardening creativity as you create a stunning focal point in your outdoor space.

3. Old metal buckets or tubs

The creative container gardening idea is to utilize old metal buckets or tubs as planters.

Materials needed:

- Old metal buckets or tubs (with drainage holes, if possible)
- Potting soil
- Assorted plants or seeds
- Watering can or spray bottle
- Fertilizer (optional)

Steps:

1. Find old metal buckets or tubs that are no longer in use and are safe for planting. Look for ones with interesting designs or rusted patinas for added character.
2. If the buckets or tubs don't already have drainage holes, use a drill to create several holes in the bottom to allow excess water to escape and prevent waterlogging.
3. Fill each bucket or tub with potting soil, leaving a few inches of space at the top for planting and watering.
4. Select a variety of plants or seeds that are suitable for container gardening and will thrive in the conditions of your outdoor space. Consider using a mix of flowering plants, herbs, or foliage plants for a dynamic and visually appealing display.
5. Plant the selected plants or sow the seeds in the buckets or tubs, following the spacing and planting depth recommendations for each plant variety. Arrange the plants creatively, considering their growth habits and the size of the containers.
6. Water the plants thoroughly after planting, ensuring the soil is evenly moist and not soggy. Use a watering can or spray bottle to water the plants gently, taking care not to overwater.
7. Place the buckets or tubs in a sunny or partially shaded location where the plants can receive adequate sunlight for healthy growth. Water the plants regularly throughout the growing season, checking the soil moisture levels weekly and watering as needed to keep the soil evenly moist.
8. Optional: Apply a balanced liquid fertilizer to the plants every few weeks to promote healthy growth and vibrant

foliage or flowers. Follow the manufacturer's instructions for application, and avoid over-fertilizing, which can lead to nutrient imbalances.
9. Enjoy the rustic charm and upcycled beauty of your metal bucket or tub planters as they add character and interest to your outdoor space. Sit back, relax, and take pride in your gardening creativity as you create a unique, eco-friendly container garden that reflects your style.

4. Old wooden crates

The creative container gardening idea is to repurpose old wooden crates as planters.

Materials needed:

- Old wooden crates
- Landscape fabric or plastic liner
- Potting soil
- Assorted plants or seeds
- Watering can or spray bottle
- Fertilizer (optional)

Steps:

1. Find old wooden crates that are sturdy and in good condition. Look for crates with slats wide enough to accommodate plants and soil.
2. Line the bottom and sides of each crate with landscape fabric or plastic liner to prevent soil from falling out and to protect the wood from moisture damage.
3. Fill each crate with potting soil, leaving a few inches of space at the top for planting and watering.
4. Select a variety of plants or seeds that are suitable for container gardening and will thrive in the conditions of your outdoor space. Consider using a mix of flowering plants, herbs, or foliage plants for a diverse and visually appealing display.
5. Plant the selected plants or sow the seeds in the crates, following the spacing and planting depth recommendations for each plant variety. Arrange the plants creatively, considering their growth habits and the size of the crates.
6. Water the plants thoroughly after planting, ensuring the soil is evenly moist and not soggy. Use a watering can or spray bottle to water the plants gently, taking care not to overwater.
7. Place the crates in a sunny or partially shaded location where the plants can receive adequate sunlight for healthy growth. Water the plants regularly throughout the growing season, checking the soil moisture levels weekly and watering as needed to keep the soil evenly moist.
8. Optional: Apply a balanced liquid fertilizer to the plants every few weeks to promote healthy growth and vibrant foliage or flowers. Follow the manufacturer's instructions

for application, and avoid over-fertilizing, which can lead to nutrient imbalances.
9. Enjoy your wooden crate planters' rustic charm and upcycled beauty as they add character and warmth to your outdoor space. Sit back, relax, and take pride in your creativity as you create a unique and sustainable container garden that reflects your style.

Chapter 7: Common Container Gardening Issues

1. Overwatering

Overwatering is a common problem in container gardening that occurs when plants receive more water than they need. This excess water can lead to various issues, including root rot, fungal diseases, and nutrient leaching. Understanding the causes and consequences of overwatering is crucial for maintaining healthy container plants.

Causes of Overwatering

- Overzealous watering: Gardeners may water their container plants too frequently, believing that more water will lead to better growth.
- Poor drainage: Containers without adequate drainage holes or with compacted soil can trap excess water, leading to waterlogging.
- Incorrect watering schedule: Inconsistent watering practices, such as irregular watering intervals or inappropriate times of day, can contribute to overwatering.

Consequences of Overwatering

- Root rot: Excess moisture in the soil suffocates plant roots, leading to root rot and eventual plant death.
- Fungal diseases: Overwatered plants are more susceptible to fungal diseases like powdery mildew and botrytis.
- Nutrient leaching: Overwatering can wash away essential nutrients from the soil, depriving plants of the nutrition they need to thrive.
- Reduced oxygen availability: Waterlogged soil lacks sufficient oxygen, impairing root function and inhibiting plant growth.

How to Solve the Problem

- Check soil moisture: Before watering, use your finger or a moisture meter to check the soil moisture level. Water only when the top inch of soil feels dry to the touch.
- Improve drainage: Ensure your containers have adequate drainage holes in the bottom to allow excess water to escape. Elevating containers on pot feet or adding a layer of gravel at the bottom can also improve drainage.
- Use well-draining soil: Choose a high-quality potting mix that is specifically formulated for container gardening and provides good drainage.
- Adjust watering schedule: Develop a consistent watering schedule based on the specific needs of your plants, considering factors such as plant type, container size, and environmental conditions. Water plants deeply but less frequently to encourage healthy root growth.
- Water at the right time: Water plants early in the morning or late in the afternoon to minimize evaporation and allow the soil to absorb moisture more effectively.
- Monitor plants closely: Monitor your container plants for signs of overwatering, such as wilting, yellowing leaves, or mold growth. Adjust your watering practices accordingly to prevent further damage.

2. Underwatering

Underwatering is another common issue in container gardening that occurs when plants do not receive enough water to meet their needs. If left unaddressed, this can lead to wilting, stunted growth, and even plant death. Understanding the causes and consequences of underwatering and how to solve the problem is essential for maintaining healthy container plants.

Causes of Underwatering

- Inconsistent watering: Gardeners may forget to water their container plants regularly or may not water deeply enough to reach the roots.
- Hot and dry conditions: Containers exposed to direct sunlight or in windy locations can dry out quickly, increasing the risk of underwatering.
- Improper container selection: Containers with small openings or limited soil volume may dry out more quickly than larger containers, leading to underwatering.

Consequences of Underwatering

- Wilting: Plants deprived of water may wilt and appear limp as they struggle to maintain turgor pressure.
- Stunted growth: Underwatered plants may exhibit slowed growth and produce fewer flowers or fruit.
- Leaf damage: Leaves may become crispy, curl, or brown at the edges due to moisture stress.

- Reduced yield: Underwatered plants may produce smaller or fewer fruits, vegetables, or flowers than adequately hydrated plants.
- Increased susceptibility to pests and diseases: Stressed plants are more vulnerable to pest infestations and diseases, which can further weaken their health and vitality.

How to Solve the Problem

- Establish a watering routine: Develop a consistent watering schedule based on the specific needs of your plants, considering factors such as plant type, container size, and environmental conditions. Water plants deeply and thoroughly to ensure the entire root zone is moistened.
- Monitor soil moisture: Check the soil moisture regularly using your finger or a moisture meter. Water plants when the top inch of soil feels dry to the touch, and adjust your watering frequency as needed based on weather conditions and plant response.
- Mulch the soil: Apply a layer of organic mulch, such as straw, wood chips, or shredded bark, to the soil's surface to help retain moisture and reduce evaporation.
- Choose appropriate containers: Use adequate drainage holes and soil volume to retain moisture and support healthy root growth. Consider using self-watering containers or adding water reservoirs to help maintain consistent soil moisture levels.
- Group plants strategically: Grouping plants with similar water requirements together in containers can help

streamline your watering routine and ensure that all plants receive the moisture they need.
- Provide shade and shelter: Place containers in shaded or sheltered locations during hot and dry periods to minimize water loss through evaporation and reduce plant stress.

3. Poor drainage

Poor drainage is a common problem in container gardening that occurs when excess water cannot drain effectively from the soil, leading to waterlogging and root suffocation. This issue can harm plant health and growth if not addressed promptly. Understanding the causes and consequences of poor drainage and how to solve the problem is essential for maintaining healthy container plants.

Causes of Poor Drainage

- Lack of drainage holes: Containers without adequate drainage holes in the bottom trap excess water, preventing it from escaping and leading to waterlogged soil.
- Compacted soil: Soil that becomes compacted over time restricts water infiltration and drainage, exacerbating drainage problems.
- Incorrect potting mix: Using heavy or dense potting mixes that retain too much moisture can contribute to poor drainage.

- Container placement: Containers placed on impervious surfaces, such as concrete or asphalt, may not allow water to drain from the soil effectively.
- Container design: Containers with narrow openings or restricted airflow may impede water drainage and ventilation, leading to moisture buildup.

Consequences of Poor Drainage

- Root suffocation: Waterlogged soil deprives plant roots of oxygen, leading to root suffocation and impaired nutrient uptake.
- Root rot: Prolonged exposure to waterlogged conditions promotes the growth of root rot pathogens, which can cause root decay and plant decline.
- Fungal diseases: Moist and stagnant conditions created by poor drainage provide an ideal environment for fungal diseases like powdery mildew and botrytis to thrive.
- Nutrient leaching: Excess water can wash away essential nutrients from the soil, leading to nutrient deficiencies and poor plant health.
- Stunted growth: Plants grown in poorly drained soil may exhibit stunted growth, yellowing leaves, and reduced vigor.

How to Solve the Problem

- Drill drainage holes: If your containers do not have drainage holes, use a drill to create several holes in the bottom to allow excess water to escape freely.
- Use well-draining potting mix: Choose a high-quality potting mix specifically formulated for container gardening that provides good drainage and aeration. Avoid heavy or clay-based soils that retain too much moisture.
- Add drainage materials: Place a layer of coarse gravel, perlite, or crushed stones at the bottom of the container before adding potting soil to improve drainage and prevent waterlogging.
- Elevate containers: Place containers on pot feet or bricks to lift them off the ground and promote airflow and drainage.
- Repot plants: If plants already suffer from poor drainage, consider repotting them into containers with better drainage or amending the soil with organic matter to improve aeration.
- Monitor soil moisture: Regularly check the soil moisture and adjust your watering practices to prevent overwatering and waterlogging.
- Improve container placement: Ensure that containers are placed on porous surfaces or elevated platforms to allow excess water to drain away from the soil effectively.

4. Soil compaction

Soil compaction is a common issue in container gardening that occurs when the soil becomes densely packed, limiting root growth, water infiltration, and nutrient absorption. This problem can harm plant health and productivity if not addressed promptly. Understanding the causes and consequences of soil compaction and how to solve the problem is crucial for maintaining healthy container plants.

Causes of Soil Compaction

- Overwatering: Excessive watering can lead to soil compaction as the weight of water compresses the soil particles, reducing pore space and air circulation.
- Foot traffic: Compaction can occur when containers are placed in high-traffic areas or when gardeners walk on the soil surface, compacting the soil with their weight.
- Heavy equipment: Using heavy equipment or tools on the soil surface, such as trowels or gardening forks, can compact the soil and damage root systems.
- Organic matter decomposition: Over time, organic matter in the soil breaks down, causing the soil to settle and become compacted.
- Lack of aeration: Soil that is not regularly aerated through natural processes or mechanical means can become compacted over time.

Consequences of Soil Compaction

- Restricted root growth: Compacted soil restricts root penetration and expansion, inhibiting the development of a healthy root system and reducing nutrient uptake.
- Impaired water infiltration: Compacted soil has reduced pore space, limiting water infiltration and drainage and increasing the risk of waterlogging and root rot.
- Nutrient deficiencies: Compacted soil impedes the movement of water and nutrients through the soil profile, leading to nutrient deficiencies and poor plant health.
- Reduced soil fertility: Soil compaction can disrupt soil microbial activity and nutrient cycling, reducing soil fertility and overall plant productivity.
- Decreased aeration: Compacted soil lacks adequate air pockets, depriving plant roots of oxygen and hindering root respiration and nutrient absorption.

How to Solve the Problem

- Loosen the soil: Use a small hand rake, fork, or aerator to gently loosen the soil surface and break up compacted areas, improving soil structure and aeration.
- Add organic matter: Incorporate organic amendments such as compost, aged manure, or peat moss into the soil to improve soil structure, water retention, and nutrient availability.
- Avoid overwatering: Water plants deeply but infrequently to avoid waterlogging and soil compaction. Allow the soil surface to dry between waterings to encourage root growth and prevent compaction.

- Mulch the soil: Apply a layer of organic mulch, such as shredded leaves or straw, to the soil surface to help maintain soil moisture, regulate temperature, and reduce compaction from foot traffic.
- Rotate containers: Rotate or move them to different locations regularly to distribute weight evenly and prevent soil compaction in specific areas.
- Use raised beds: Use raised or elevated containers with loose, well-draining soil to minimize soil compaction and promote healthy root growth.
- Avoid compacting the soil: Avoid walking or standing on the soil surface, especially when wet, to prevent soil compaction and damage to plant roots.

5. Nutrient deficiency

Nutrient deficiency is a common issue in container gardening that occurs when plants do not receive an adequate supply of essential nutrients required for healthy growth and development. This problem can arise due to various factors, including poor soil quality, leaching of nutrients, and imbalanced fertilization practices. Understanding the causes and consequences of nutrient deficiency and how to solve the problem is crucial for maintaining healthy container plants.

Causes of Nutrient Deficiency

- Poor soil quality: Container plants rely on potting mix for their nutrient supply, and low-quality or depleted soil may lack essential nutrients necessary for plant growth.
- Leaching of nutrients: Watering container plants can lead to the leaching of nutrients from the soil, especially in containers with inadequate drainage or during heavy rainfall.
- Imbalanced fertilization: Overusing or underusing fertilizers and using the wrong type of fertilizer can lead to nutrient imbalances and deficiencies in container plants.
- pH imbalance: Soil pH can affect nutrient availability to plants, and extreme pH levels can interfere with nutrient uptake and lead to deficiencies.
- Plant uptake: Some plants have higher nutrient requirements than others, and certain environmental conditions or stressors can increase nutrient demands, leading to deficiencies.

Consequences of Nutrient Deficiency

- Stunted growth: Nutrient-deficient plants may exhibit slowed growth, smaller leaves, and reduced vigor compared to healthy plants.
- Yellowing leaves: Yellowing or chlorosis of leaves is a common symptom of nutrient deficiency, indicating a lack of essential nutrients such as nitrogen, iron, or magnesium.

- Poor fruit or flower production: Nutrient deficiencies can impair flowering and fruiting in plants, leading to reduced yields and poor-quality produce.
- Susceptibility to pests and diseases: Nutrient-deficient plants are more vulnerable to pest infestations and diseases due to weakened immune systems and reduced resistance to stressors.
- Leaf discoloration: Nutrient deficiencies can cause characteristic leaf discoloration patterns, such as brown or purple spots, interveinal chlorosis, or leaf curling.

How to Solve the Problem

- Test the soil: Conduct a soil test to determine nutrient levels and pH in the potting mix. Soil tests can help identify specific nutrient deficiencies and guide fertilization practices.
- Use balanced fertilizers: Choose a balanced fertilizer specifically formulated for container plants and apply it according to the manufacturer's instructions. Look for fertilizers with a balanced N-P-K ratio (nitrogen, phosphorus, potassium) and micronutrients.
- Foliar feeding: Apply liquid fertilizers or nutrient solutions directly to the leaves of plants as a supplement to soil fertilization to provide a quick boost of nutrients.
- Amend the soil: Incorporate organic matter, such as compost or aged manure, into the potting mix to improve soil fertility and nutrient retention.
- Adjust pH: If soil pH is imbalanced, amend the soil with pH-adjusting amendments such as lime (to raise pH) or

sulfur (to lower pH) to optimize nutrient availability to plants.
- Monitor plant health: Regularly inspect plants for signs of nutrient deficiency, such as leaf discoloration or poor growth, and address deficiencies promptly with appropriate fertilization or soil amendments.
- Maintain proper watering and drainage: Ensure container plants receive adequate water and proper drainage to prevent nutrient leaching and maintain optimal soil moisture levels.

6. Root-Bound Plants

Root-bound plants occur when the roots of container-grown plants become overcrowded and begin to circle the inside of the pot. This condition can lead to stunted growth, nutrient deficiencies, and an overall decline in plant health if left unaddressed. Understanding the causes and consequences of root-bound plants and how to solve the problem is essential for maintaining healthy container plants.

Causes of Root-Bound Plants

- Limited space: Plants grown in containers eventually outgrow their pots, and if not repotted into larger containers, their roots become confined and overcrowded.
- Infrequent repotting: Failure to repot container plants into larger containers as they grow leads to restricted root growth and root-bound conditions.

- Dense potting mix: Heavy or compacted mixes can impede root penetration and cause roots to circle within the pot, contributing to root-bound plants.
- Overgrown root systems: Some plants are more prone to developing dense root systems that quickly fill the container and become root-bound.
- Container design: Containers with narrow openings or restricted space for root expansion can accelerate the development of root-bound plants.

Consequences of Root-Bound Plants

- Stunted growth: Root-bound plants may exhibit slowed growth and reduced vigor due to restricted root growth and nutrient uptake.
- Nutrient deficiencies: Overcrowded roots compete for limited nutrients in the soil, leading to nutrient deficiencies and poor plant health.
- Water stress: Root-bound plants may struggle to absorb water efficiently, leading to uneven soil moisture levels, wilting, and water stress.
- Pot-bound root system: Over time, root-bound plants may develop a dense mass of circling roots that can strangle and inhibit healthy root growth.
- Reduced flowering or fruiting: Root-bound plants may produce fewer flowers or fruit than healthy plants due to restricted root growth and nutrient uptake.

How to Solve the Problem

- Repot into larger containers: Transplant root-bound plants into larger containers with adequate space for root expansion. Choose containers that are 1-2 inches larger in diameter than the current pot.
- Loosen roots: Before repotting, gently loosen the root ball to encourage outward root growth and prevent circling roots. Use your fingers to tease apart compacted roots or make shallow cuts along the root ball with a knife.
- Amend potting mix: Use a high-quality, well-draining mix with a balanced blend of organic matter and perlite or vermiculite to promote healthy root growth.
- Prune roots: If root-bound plants have a dense mass of circling roots, carefully trim away the outer layer of roots to encourage new root growth and prevent pot-bound conditions.
- Provide proper care: After repotting, water the plant thoroughly and monitor soil moisture levels closely to ensure that the plant receives adequate hydration. Avoid overwatering or underwatering; both can stress the plant and hinder root growth.
- Maintain appropriate container size: Regularly check container size and repot plants into larger containers as needed to prevent root-bound conditions from occurring in the future.
- Monitor plant health: Keep an eye on the plant for signs of stress, such as wilting, yellowing leaves, or reduced growth, and take appropriate action to address any issues promptly.

7. Diseases

Diseases are a common problem in container gardening, caused by fungal, bacterial, or viral pathogens that infect plants and cause various symptoms such as wilting, leaf spots, rotting, and stunted growth. These diseases can spread rapidly in the confined space of containers, especially when environmental conditions favor pathogen growth. Understanding the causes and consequences of diseases in container gardening and how to solve the problem is essential for maintaining healthy plants.

Causes of Diseases in Container Gardening

- Pathogen presence: Fungal, bacterial, and viral pathogens can be present in the potting mix, on plant debris, or in contaminated water sources and can infect plants when conditions are conducive to their growth.
- High humidity: Warm, humid conditions create an ideal environment for disease development and spread, especially in the confined space of containers.
- Overcrowding: Overcrowded containers can promote disease spread by creating favorable conditions for pathogen growth and limiting airflow around plants.
- Poor sanitation: Contaminated tools, pots, and equipment can introduce pathogens to container plants and contribute to disease spread.
- Imbalanced watering: Overwatering or underwatering can stress plants and weaken their immune systems, making them more susceptible to disease infection.

Consequences of Diseases in Container Gardening

- Reduced plant vigor: Diseased plants may exhibit reduced growth, wilting, and overall decline in vigor due to the damage caused by pathogens.
- Poor fruit or flower production: Disease-infected plants may produce fewer flowers or fruits than healthy plants, leading to reduced yields and poor-quality produce.
- Spread to other plants: Diseases can spread rapidly in container gardens, infecting neighboring plants through water splashes, contaminated soil, or shared tools and equipment.
- Loss of harvest: Severe disease outbreaks can lead to crop loss or complete plant death, resulting in loss of time, effort, and resources invested in container gardening.
- Environmental impact: Chemical fungicides and pesticides used to control diseases in container gardening can negatively affect the environment and beneficial organisms.

How to Solve the Problem

- Practice good sanitation: Regularly clean and disinfect tools, pots, and equipment to prevent the spread of pathogens between plants. Remove and dispose of diseased plant debris promptly to reduce disease pressure.
- Use disease-resistant varieties: Choose plant varieties resistant to common diseases in your area to minimize

the risk of infection and reduce the need for chemical controls.
- Improve airflow: Space containers apart to improve airflow around plants and reduce humidity levels, inhibiting disease development and spread.
- Water plants carefully: Water plants at the base to avoid wetting foliage, as wet leaves provide a favorable environment for disease development. Use drip irrigation or soaker hoses to deliver water directly to the soil.
- Provide proper drainage: Ensure containers have adequate drainage to prevent waterlogging and reduce the risk of root rot and other soil-borne diseases.
- Monitor plant health: Regularly inspect plants for signs of disease, such as yellowing leaves, leaf spots, or mold growth, and promptly address any issues. Remove and dispose of diseased plant material to prevent further spread of infection.
- Use organic controls: Employ cultural practices such as crop rotation, companion planting, and mulching to promote plant health and reduce disease pressure naturally. Consider using organic fungicides and biological controls as alternatives to chemical treatments when necessary.

Conclusion

Container gardening offers a flexible and rewarding way to cultivate plants in various spaces, from small balconies and patios to expansive gardens. As we conclude our exploration of container gardening, it's evident that this method provides numerous benefits and opportunities for gardeners of all experience levels.

Firstly, container gardening allows for maximum flexibility in plant selection and placement. Regardless of space limitations or soil quality, gardeners can grow various plants, including flowers, herbs, vegetables, and even small trees and shrubs. This versatility makes container gardening accessible to urban dwellers, renters, and anyone with limited outdoor space.

Container gardening offers greater control over growing conditions, including soil composition, drainage, and exposure to sunlight. Gardeners can customize potting mixes, choose containers with adequate drainage, and position plants to optimize sunlight exposure, ensuring optimal plant growth conditions.

Furthermore, container gardening provides opportunities for creativity and personalization. Gardeners can experiment with different container materials, shapes, and sizes and mix and match plants to create unique and visually appealing container arrangements. Whether it's a vibrant display of flowers on a balcony or a bountiful vegetable garden on a patio, container gardening allows gardeners to express their styles and preferences.

Moreover, container gardening promotes sustainability and resource conservation. Using recycled materials, conserving water through drip irrigation or self-watering containers, and growing edible plants at home, container gardeners can reduce their environmental footprint and contribute to a more sustainable lifestyle.

In conclusion, container gardening is a versatile, accessible, and rewarding method that empowers gardeners to grow plants in various spaces and environments. Whether you're a seasoned gardener looking to expand your growing space or a novice gardener eager to start your gardening journey, container gardening offers endless possibilities for creativity, productivity, and enjoyment. So grab your pots, potting mix, and plants, and embark on your container gardening adventure today!

Printed in Great Britain
by Amazon